The Turtle Who Went to War

and Other Sioux Stories

The Turtle Who Went to War

and Other Sioux Stories

Published by the
Montana Historical Society Press
in cooperation with the
Fort Peck Assiniboine and Sioux Tribes

HELENA, MONTANA

Originally published as *The Turtle Who Went to War, Sioux Stories and Legends,* and *White Rabbit* in the Indian Reading Series by the Pacific Northwest Indian Program, Joseph Coburn, Director, Northwest Regional Educational Laboratory, Portland, Oregon

Cover drawing by Lisa Ventura
Design by DD Dowden

Revised edition copyright © 2003 by Fort Peck Tribal Library, Fort Peck Community College, P.O. Box 398, Poplar, Montana 59255

Distributed by the Globe Pequot Press, 246 Goose Lane, Guilford, Connecticut 06437, (800) 243-0495

Library of Congress Cataloging-in-Publication Data:
The turtle who went to war : and other Sioux stories.
      p. cm.
Summary: A collection of five traditional tales, told and illustrated by Indians living at Fort Peck reservation in northern Montana, which reveal the Sioux culture.
Contents: The turtle who went to war—Moosehide Robe Woman—Pet crow—Owl boy—White rabbit.
ISBN 0-917298-95-0 (pbk. : alk. paper)
1. Dakota Indians—Folklore. 2. Assiniboine Indians—Folklore. 3. Tales—Montana—Fort Peck Indian Reservation. 4. Legends—Montana—Fort Peck Indian reservation. [1. Dakota Indians—Folklore. 2. Indians of North America—Montana—Folklore. 3. Folklore—Montana.]
E99.D1T87 2003
398.2'089'9752—dc21

                              2003044555

The Turtle Who Went to War copyright © 1978 by the Assiniboine and Sioux Tribes of the Fort Peck Reservation

Sioux Stories and Legends (which includes "Mooseshide Robe Woman," "Pet Crow," and "Owl Boy") and *White Rabbit* copyright © 1981 by the Assiniboine and Sioux Tribes of the Fort Peck Reservation

This project was funded by an Enhancement Grant from the
Institute of Museum and Library Services awarded
to Fort Peck Tribal Library in 2001.
Additional funding was provided by
Assiniboine and Sioux Enterprise Community

CONTENTS

The Turtle Who Went to War

As told by Lavina Perry
Illustrated by Lisa Ventura

THIS SIOUX STORY TELLS HOW ONCE, long ago, the Turtles decided to go on a warpath against the Indians. The Indians had been greedy and had killed too many Turtles to eat, which made the Turtle chief very angry. So, the Turtles went on a warpath and killed the Indian chief.

There once was a large camp of Water Turtles. One day, the chief of the Turtles sent around the pipe to all the friendly tribes—the Grasshoppers, Butterflies, Frogs, Snakes and Rabbits. The chiefs smoked the pipe. Then they sent their young men to the Turtle chief, who spoke to them. "There are many Indians camped nearby," he said. "Let's go on the warpath and kill their chief." They all said they would go on the warpath.

The warriors walked around the inside of the camp circle and went out the opening to the east. Then they walked around the outside of the camp and started off, carrying their war bonnets and war clothes. They walked all night. Just before the sun came up, they reached the Indian camp. The warriors attacked. The Turtle chief went into the Indian chief's lodge. The Turtle took the Indian by the throat and choked him until he was dead. He bit off the scalp and slipped under the dead chief's bed.

Later that morning, the Indians found their dead chief. A crier went through the camp, telling the people to watch out for enemies. Later, someone moved the chief's bed and saw a spot of fresh earth under it. Pushing a stick into the earth, he felt the Turtle. Then the Indians knew that the Turtle had killed their chief.

The people wondered what they should do with the Turtle. "Put him in the fire," said one man. "No," said another, "we can't burn him. His shell is too hard. Let's hang him." "No, let's cut off his head," said another. "No," said a fourth man, "let's drown him." Everyone thought that was the best way.

The next afternoon, the Indians took the Turtle to a pond. A crowd of people followed, for they wanted to see him killed. A man was chosen to drown the Turtle. The man was painted with war paint. Carrying the Turtle, he waded out to the center of the pond. The Turtle shook and acted like he was very frightened. But as the man started to put him into the water, the Turtle turned his head and bit him! The man jumped and fell into the water. The Turtle drowned the Indian and bit off his scalp.

When the man didn't come to the top of the water, the people didn't know what to do. They were afraid to go into the water, so they left. The Turtle stayed in the pond until night came. Then he went back to the Indian camp and hunted until he found the chief's scalp.

The Turtle was glad that he had taken the two scalps by himself. He started home.

Moosehide Robe Woman

As told by George White Bird
Illustrated by LaVern Alfrey

Moosehide Robe Woman was an only child. Her parents loved her very much. They let Moosehide Robe Woman do whatever she wanted to do.

Every night young men would come to see Moosehide Robe Woman. They all wanted to marry her. Moosehide Robe Woman didn't like most of the young men. She only cared for two certain men.

One night Moosehide Robe Woman followed the first man to his tepee. She found that this young man was very spoiled and mean to his mother.

On another night, she went to the second man's tepee. She saw that he was kind to his mother.

Moosehide Robe Woman decided to marry the second man. His name was Star Boy.

The following morning Moosehide Robe Woman was
going to tell her parents she wanted to marry Star Boy.
Before she could tell her parents, she was interrupted
by the chief.

The chief told all the young warriors to get ready for a
long journey. The warriors were going to do battle with
their enemies. The next day Star Boy and all the other
young men left the camp.

Moosehide Robe Woman decided to follow Star boy.

When Moosehide Robe Woman followed the warriors, she stayed far behind them. When the men finally saw Moosehide Robe Woman, Star Boy tried to tell her to return home, but she told Star Boy she wanted to stay with him. Moosehide Robe Woman didn't care if it was dangerous. She said she would hide.

The next morning the warriors found the enemy. Star Boy's leg was wounded. He was captured and taken to the enemy's camp.

That night, Moosehide Robe Woman followed the enemy to their camp. She searched and searched for Star Boy. When Moosehide Robe Woman found Star Boy, she helped him to escape.

After Moosehide Robe Woman and Star Boy were far
away from the camp, they hid in some bushes. Soon the
enemy warriors were near. They looked for Moosehide
Robe Woman and Star Boy but could not find them.

Many days passed. Because Star Boy and Moosehide Robe
Woman did not return home, everyone thought they had
been killed in battle. Their parents were very sad.

Star Boy and Moosehide Robe Woman took a long time
because many days passed before Star Boy was able to
walk. With the help of Moosehide Robe Woman, Star Boy
used a crutch to travel. Together, they walked back to
their camp.

One night, Star Boy and Moosehide Robe Woman finally
reached their camp. Everyone was surprised and their
parents were very happy.

Star Boy told everyone how brave Moosehide Robe Woman had been. He told of how she had rescued him from the enemy's camp. Everyone was so happy they celebrated with a feast.

Moosehide Robe Woman and Star Boy lived a long and happy life.

Pet Crow

As told by Eunice B. Alfrey
Illustrated by LaVern Alfrey

Many years ago, there lived a great chief. One day
when the chief was hunting, he found a crow. The crow
was hurt with a broken wing. The chief took the crow
home and cared for it.

When the crow's wing was better,
the bird was taught to speak.
Soon the crow could talk and
understand the language of
the tribe. The crow understood
everything the chief told him.

The chief told the bird to spy on people.
These people were enemies
of the chief. The crow
would go to the
enemies' camps
and learn all their
secrets. When
the crow returned
home, he would
tell the chief all
of the secrets.

Soon the chief won
many battles. All of
the chief's enemies
were afraid of him.

One day the crow returned home with sad news. He told the chief a great medicine man had put a curse on him. The crow said a bolt of lightning would kill him.

All of the people were very sad. They knew something terrible was going to happen.

A storm came and the sky became very dark. Rain fell and thunder and lightning struck everywhere.

People ran and hid in their tepees. Even the chief and crow hid in their tepee. Everyone was afraid of the storm.

Early the next morning the people woke up. The storm had stopped. The people heard the crow's lonely cry. They found the chief's burned tepee. The chief had been hit by a lightning bolt.

The people saw that the crow had been burned. They watched the bird fly away and listened to his lonely cries.

Today, some people say the crow is black because he was burned long, long ago.

Owl Boy

As told and illustrated by Eunice B. Alfrey

Long, long ago Indian people would hunt buffalo. The people would follow the buffalo herds. One of the Indian hunters had a wife a one-year-old son.

One day the hunter's son became very sick. The boy's body shook and shivered, then lay very still. The mother and father thought their son had died.

The little boy's parents were very sad. They made an Indian burial platform on top of four poles. They placed the boy's body on top of the platform.

After everyone had gone the little boy woke up. He began to cry. A man owl and his wife were flying nearby. They heard the boy crying and helped him down.

The owls took the boy to their nest. They cared for the little boy like their own son. The wise old owl taught the boy lessons every day. As the boy grew up, he learned many things.

One day, the owl could see that the boy was very sad. He knew the boy wanted to see his people and family. The owl and his wife decided to help the boy find his parents. They told the boy they would show him the way.

The owls flew above the boy and helped guide him. They traveled for three days. When they found the camp, the boy could not speak to the people. Every time he talked, the people could not understand him. The boy drew pictures to show how the owls had found him. The people saw the pictures and the parents knew the boy was their own.

Everyone was happy. The boy lived with his family and tribe for the rest of his life.

White Rabbit

Written by Ann Lambert
Illustrated by Joseph Clancy

Long ago there lived a chief and his wife. The chief's name was Mad Bear. He was big, strong and quite handsome. Mad Bear was a very wise and kindhearted chief. His wife's name was Gives Away White Horses Woman. Everyone in the tribe call her White Horse Woman. She was very small and beautiful with long pretty hair the color of midnight. White Horse Woman was very quiet. When she did speak, her voice was so soft the words were almost a whisper. She was a very kind and gentle woman.

The chief and his wife longed to have a child. White Horse Woman often became very sad when she watched the children in the camp playing. Their joyful laughter often made her weep. She loved the children very much. Great Spirit, however, had not given her and Mad Bear a child to love and care for. White Horse Woman's unhappiness caused Mad Bear to feel great sadness. He tried to comfort her but she became more lonely as the seasons passed.

One beautiful summer day, as White Horse Woman and the other women of the camp were picking chokecherries, she saw a little white rabbit. The little rabbit sat beside the chokecherry bush and did not move. The little animal seemed to be lost and very much afraid. "Poor little rabbit, have you lost your mother?" White Horse Woman asked as she knelt down beside it.

The little white rabbit slowly lifted its head and sadly gazed at White Horse Woman. A tear began to trickle down from the corner of the rabbit's eye. The little rabbit seemed to say, "Yes, I am lost and very much afraid."

White Horse woman said, "Poor little rabbit, I shall take you back to our camp. I will feed you and care for you. You will bring much joy and laughter."

As she spoke to the little rabbit, it hopped toward her. White Horse Woman began to laugh. The little rabbit sensed her kindness and seemed to no longer be afraid. White Horse Woman picked up the little white rabbit and cuddled it in her arms. "I shall show you to the chief and the children," she said. "They will be so pleased that I have found you."

Many of the children were playing by a stream. White Horse Woman called to them, "Come and see what I have found." The children became very excited. "Don't frighten the little rabbit," White Horse Woman told the children.

They followed White Horse Woman and the rabbit back to camp. As they approached, their laughter could be heard by the elders, who were always pleased when they saw the children in a happy mood. White Horse Woman told the children, "I will take the little white rabbit into my tepee and feed it. After the poor little animal has rested, we shall let it become familiar with its new home and friends."

White Horse Woman took the little white rabbit into her tepee and gently laid it on a soft buffalo robe. The little rabbit seemed to smile at her with its big eyes. "Little white rabbit," she said, "how I would love to have a child as beautiful and gentle as you."

As she spoke the chief walked inside. "My wife, what have you found?" he asked.

She told him of how she and the little white rabbit had come to meet. Mad Bear saw the happiness in White Horse Woman's eyes. Many seasons had passed since she last displayed so much joy. His heart filled with loving happiness. How he hoped and prayed the Great Spirit would soon bless them with a child who would bring them as much happiness.

As the days passed, the little white rabbit came to know the children. They played with it but were careful not to hurt it. The little white rabbit grew as the days passed.

One day White Horse Woman told the children, "Because little white rabbit has grown, we shall have to call it White Rabbit. It is not a little white rabbit anymore." The children thought it should be so. From then on the rabbit was called White Rabbit.

One beautiful autumn evening, White Rabbit hopped into White Horse Woman's tepee. White Rabbit began to hop and dance on the soft buffalo robe. White Horse Woman began to laugh and sing. She and White Rabbit had come to love each other very much. White Rabbit had become her special friend.

White Rabbit lay down on the buffalo robe and looked sadly into White Horse Woman's eyes. The rabbit sensed her heart was still filled with sadness. White Horse Woman spoke to White Rabbit. "Yes, my friend, I am still very sad. The Great Spirit has not yet answered our prayers. Mad Bear says we must be patient. The Great Spirit will choose the time to give us our child. But so many seasons have passed. White Rabbit, you must help me be patient."

White Rabbit hopped on White Horse Woman's lap and snuggled into her arms. "What a true friend you are," she told White Rabbit. "I will be patient and continue to pray to the Great Spirit."

One season had passed since White Rabbit was brought to the camp. For a reason she could not explain, White Horse Woman sensed that White Rabbit soon would leave them. A great sadness filled her heart, but she knew that animals and birds were meant to be free. Every living being needed some freedom. The Great Spirit said it was so, and for this reason, she could not force White Rabbit to stay.

The following night, as White Horse Woman slept, she dreamed of White Rabbit. In her dream White Rabbit was playing with the children. White Rabbit was hopping and dancing with the children. The children began dancing in a circle around White Rabbit. As White Rabbit joyfully hopped, a cloud formed around it. It was very difficult to see White Rabbit.

Suddenly, the children's laughter became louder and louder. As they drew away from the circle, White Horse Woman saw the figure of the most beautiful little girl she had ever seen. The little girl wore a white buckskin dress with long fringes. Her hair was long and the color of midnight. Her eyes were very large, brown and filled with happiness. The little girl turned and looked at White Horse Woman. She called her "Mother" in a tone that was but a whisper. White Horse Woman woke Mad Bear and told him of her dream. It had made her so very happy.

The sun was rising and people began their daily activities. Some of the children began looking for White Rabbit. But White Rabbit could not be found. White Horse Woman and the children became very sad. They knew their friend would never return. White Horse Woman whispered, "Be safe White Rabbit. You have been my true friend. I shall not forget you."

Another season passed. The long winter was over and spring had now shown the signs of a beautiful year. Mad Bear and his hunting party were leaving to hunt game for the people. The women, children and elders stayed in the camp and attended to their daily duties. Several days passed. Mad Bear and his hunting parties returned to camp. As they approached, they could hear joyful laughter. The men hurried to reach the camp.

Many women were gathered at Mad Bear's and White Horse Woman's tepee. Mad Bear rushed inside and found White Horse Woman sitting on her soft buffalo robe.

"My wife, what is the reason for all this joy?" he asked. Her face flowed with happiness as she spoke. "The Great Spirit has chosen this time to give us our child."

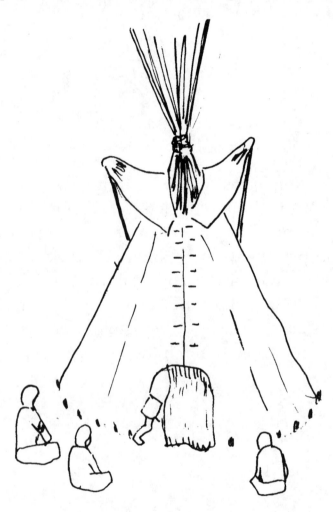

She and Mad Bear began to laugh and cry with joy. The Great Spirit was going to bless them with a child. Many seasons had passed and now they would soon have their long awaited child.

It was now late fall, and three elderly women were caring for White Horse Woman inside her tepee. The child would soon be born. Outside, Mad Bear and the others waited patiently. Suddenly, they heard a faint, then louder cry. Mad Bear was now a father.

Mad Bear was allowed to go into the tepee and join White Horse Woman and their new daughter. How beautiful she was with hair the color of midnight and eyes large and brown.

Together, Mad Bear and White Horse Woman prayed and gave thanks to the Great Spirit.

Several mornings passed and White Horse Woman
decided to take her daughter for a walk along the stream.
As she approached the stream, she noticed a white rabbit
sitting beside a chokecherry bush. White Horse Woman
slowly walked toward the rabbit.

 "Yes, my friend, the Great Spirit has been good to us,"
she spoke softly. She held the child beside the rabbit.
"You see how beautiful she is? Her name shall be White
Rabbit Woman. Your story shall be told to her children
and all their descendants."

The rabbit looked up at her and
seemed to say, "Yes, White Horse
Woman, you are kind and gentle.
You were patient."

White Horse Woman stood up and began to walk away. She whispered softly, "Be safe, White Rabbit! You have been my true friend. I shall not forget you."

White Horse Woman did not turn around. She knew White Rabbit was no longer sitting there, but it had heard her, just as the Great Spirit had heard her.

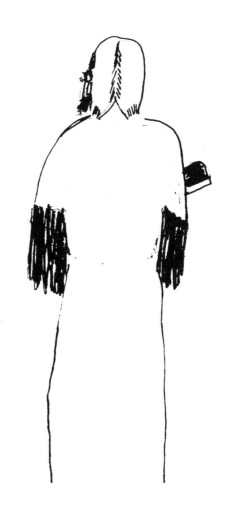

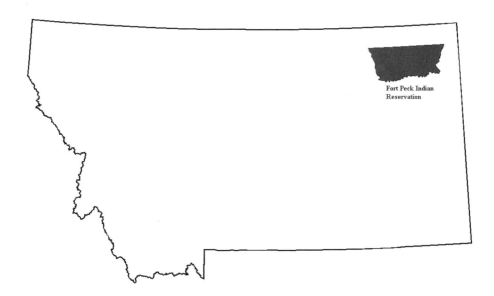

Fort Peck Indian
Reservation

About the Fort Peck Sioux

Pushed westward as Europeans began displacing Indians in the East, members of the Yanktonai, Sisseton Wahpeton, Oglala and Hunkpapa bands of Sioux came to Montana, Wyoming, Nebraska, South Dakota and North Dakota in the mid–1800s. Determined to retain their traditional ways, they battled other tribes for control of prime hunting land, successfully controlling a large territory.

Tribal members hunted buffalo and other game, fished the rivers and lakes, and gathered the many roots and fruit that the land provided. The Sioux became known for fierce resistance to white incursion, including their victory, with the Cheyenne and Assiniboine, at the Battle of the Little Bighorn. Ultimately, however, members of the tribes were moved onto reservations, including the Fort Peck Indian Reservation in northwestern Montana.

The stories published here have helped keep Sioux culture alive. Traditionally told around the fire on cold, winter evenings, stories like these were intended to help educate young tribal members about their history and culture. Children learned the stories from their elders, and, in their turn, passed them along to their children. Through this book these stories are now available to a new generation of Sioux children on the Fort Peck Indian Reservation and to children everywhere who are interested in learning about the traditional values and lifeways of the Sioux.